The Scribbling Woman

Love, Heartbreak and Poetry

Ashley Davidson

The Scribbling Woman
Love, Heartbreak and Poetry
© 2024 by Ashley Davidson

First Edition, 2024
ISBN 978-0-9977884-4-0

Printed in the United Staes of America

Social Media: @iashleydavidson

This book is dedicated to anyone
who has ever known love.

CONTENTS

This Thing Called Love

Barren and untouched
Yet, I know
I can feel it
I close my eyes and I can see it
I know it
I know her
I've seen her
Flaming in the eyes of others
Portrayed passionately upon the screen
Recited eloquently in verse and rhyme
But I've never met her face to face
Introductions have not been made
I hope my time is coming
So, I can know this thing called love

New World

A tidal wave sweeps me up
And I can't tell the floor from the ceiling
I'm overpowered and lost in its infinite waves
Able to unleash and let loose
My unbridled passions and desires
For the first time
As time itself is lost
And all coherent thought is
Unrecognizable
As I swivel and swirl
Through these uncharted waters
Tossing and turning as though in convulsions
As the wetness splashes
Upon my neck
And tickles the tops of my bosom
Playing with my senses
Relentlessly
Opening up a world I've always
Dreamed of
But never set eyes on
That is until now
Now that my feet are on the ceiling
And my head on the floor

My heart is open
And running over with thoughts of you
And overflowing with the feel of you
As sounds I've never heard before
Are slicing through the waves
And echoing in my ear
Over and over again
And I can't help to have fallen
In love with this new world
And I hope that its existence
Will last forever
And it will be waiting for me to
Rediscover a million times over
Because I am unsure
That I will ever be able to get my fill
Of this wondrous place
That has been opened to me
And I know that this is only
Just the beginning

Rejection

I approach
You repress
You dismiss my address
While all I want to do is confess
My feelings for you
And profess three words to you
That I want to express
From my heart with much success
So, you can see how much I want to impress
And love you with finesse
Because you suppress all the stress in the world
And when I'm with you I don't second guess what's
before me
Or which move to make in the life of chess
And relive the youthful days of recess
And excess joy fills me
As I hope to stand before you in my wedding dress
But oh, I digress
I just long for the simplicity of standing beside you
And to feel your tender caress
But more or less
All I really want
Is for you to look at me

And just say yes

I'm Ready

Who are you I wonder
You walked in undetected
By my watchful, vigilant eye
You sit there quietly
Loudly, hilariously and seriously
You've been here all this time
And I was never notified
You're on your side of the room
And I'm on mine
Together and yet separate
Here but not present
Alive but not existing
Who are you?
I look at you without seeing you
I hear you without listening to you
I touch you without feeling you
And I never try to know you
We are two bodies living in an
Unfamiliar space that I am desperately
Trying to make familiar
You are out of focus
As I try to focus
On the things which will bring me into focus

And that is all that I can see
Until the day that you kissed me
And my eyelids flapped open
My ears unclogged
My fingers were set ablaze
And I could feel everything
Around me take flight and
Lift me up from my rooted spot
And I saw you for the first time
My heart has been dusted off
And you have done the cleaning
I want to know you now
I want to know all that I can
At long last I'm ready for you
And I'm ready for what we can be
together

Suffering

A trail of tears are left behind
A culmination of grief and heartache follow
Her name is whispered in the dark
While her hands squeeze the heart
Blood does not taint her coat
But rather blends in improving the attire
Culpable she is though penitent she is not
Without a care in the world
She releases her venom with no restraints
Her victims fall by the way side
And she steps back to the other side
Watching as they fall
Though completely evil she may seem
Completely evil she is not
So, fear not
Because in this darkness there is a small glimmer of
hope
That few can see
For though this fall lands you on the ground
On the ground is where you ought to be
From the ground is where you learn to stand
From the ground is where you discover your purpose
She forces you to the ground

You suffer
But then you rise
You stand tall and move on

It's in Your Walk

I saw you enter the room
Right foot
Left foot
Making your presence known with your confident
stride
One, two, step
Your graceful walk hypnotizes me
Causing me to stare mindlessly
At the beautiful sight before me
You traverse the room smoothly
Inviting all eyes to see
As your right foot strokes the ground briefly
Your left foot falls with poise and elegance neatly
As it teasingly caresses the floor
My eyes begin to explore
Your charming countenance
Followed by your anatomical vibrance
I watch as your joints bend perfectly
Causing the thigh and calf to hold conversation
shortly
And your muscles tighten forcefully.

Your arms are at peace

Moving to a beat that will never cease
There's so many unspoken words, feelings and
emotions
In your refined swagger
It's like a work of art
I think I can hear and see it all
As you glide past the barriers of my heart
I love the way you walk
I love the way your body sways to the soft melodies
of the wind
Around every bend
I can feel what your presence does to me within
I love it when you're walking
Walking to the place your heart wants to be
When you're walking
Walking towards me

Betrayal

Before you pick that knife up
Let me turn around and adjust myself
So, you can get your aim right
In between the shoulder blades
At a slight 45 degree angle
More than halfway up the posterior side
I believe that would be the appropriate stabbing place
Better yet, let me turn around
Facing you head on
Now you move slightly to my right
A little more
There, now you can get me in the center of my heart
You can watch as my face
Contorts and my body writhes
And my breath is snuffed out under the excruciating
pain
You'll have a clear view and easy access
That way your job won't be so hard
So, pick up the knife
And let me know if today
You want to stab me in the back or the heart

Appetite for You

You were so close to me that I could breathe you in
I inhale deeply
Filling my lungs with your fragrance from within
Making me shiver and softly scream
Realizing it was the same sweet scent that lingers in
my dreams
You are refreshing to my senses
Making me rethink my convictions
Wanting these appetizing conditions
To occur and release all my tension
And confirm my good opinions of you and I
Sharing the breath of love together
As I inhale your soul
I begin to lose control

My hunger for you is constantly growing
As the pleasing fumes
That you bring to the room
Are swirling before me
As I take them in knowingly
And try to hold myself together controllably
With your beautiful presence glowing
And our loving words flowing

Making me desire you all the more
Evident by the smile on my face now showing
I'm savoring the essence of you
From the outline of your face
To the strength of your character base
And not to mention your masculine grace
That has me intoxicated with love
Indicative of all the joy
Peace
Confidence
Genuine happiness
And all of the above
Which you bring me
Show me
Inspire me
Fill me with
Proving that true love is not a myth
But a sense of belonging and purpose raised to the
fifth
Which is why I desire to be close to you
Gulping every good deed
And kind word you relinquish
You are the fulfillment of my wish
Putting me in a permanent state of bliss
You have quenched my thirst
And helped me survive the worst

Nursed my wounds
And stayed with me until
The flowers finally bloomed

I inhale deeply
Realizing that you are my delight
You have made the love in my
Heart forever bright
So, thank you
For satisfying my appetite

Truth

I give my love to you
And it's returned to sender
I ask for your love in return
And you refuse to surrender
I offer you all that I have
And you jump on tender
My heart is broken into pieces
And I'm off balance at my center
My pain is real and intense
Everyday January thru December
You're off being happy and content
While I'm weighed down because I remember
Every smile and warm embrace
Which equate to an eternal splendor
But now I finally see the truth
True love is the real pretender

Honey

People swarm to you like bees to honey
All the girls wish they could call you honey
But that name is reserved for me
You respond only if that
Sweetness proceeds from my lips
So even if girls wiggle their hips
Or wish to leave a tip
For a dose of honey
I won't trip
Because I know you won't slip
Or lose grip
On what we have
Because those girls aren't even equipped
To dip into the pot of honey
Our honey, honey
So, they can swarm and buzz
To their hearts content and never flee
Because I know I'm your queen bee
And I'm not worried about the other bees
Whoever they be
Because the honey pot between
You and me is not a waste
It's what most want to embrace

But some realize they can't stand the taste
But that's not the case
Between you and me
For this sweet nectar that exists
Puts me in such a state of bliss
Making my mind delirious
It's the perfect dish
Like a hot kiss upon my flesh
That I don't want to miss
But wish for again and again
Hoping that it will never end
For that would be a sin
So, we must keep the pot full
And all in the world will be cool
As for now
I wish to return to my state of bliss
So please, whisk me away, away
Away to my honey

Nothing at All

Why do you muffle my cries and ignore my calls
Why do you stand so tall
And make me feel so small
I thought you were lifting me up
But you were really letting me fall
You used to be so near to me
So dear to me
And now you can't even recall
Who I am
What we once were
The friendship that came to be
I guess it no longer is to be
At least in reference to me
But in reference to you
The friendship is not what it claimed to be
You have become someone unknown to me
And ashamed to say I knew
But let me not stall
And relay the facts to you
I guess our friendship won't survive
The long haul
I guess it was really nothing
Nothing at all

Everlasting Love

The words I love you escape from my lips
I love you too replies from your heart
We bathe in our love for each other
Joining together forever
Embracing one another with love

Our love will never get old or rotten
It shall forever be gold and never forgotten
It shall be sweet, vibrant
And in sight for all to see
It shall be with us unceasingly
Surviving even as we dream and scheme
And heaven forbid become no longer a team
It lives on and shall forever beam
Its bright light full of exuberance and hope
That you and I
Will be together until we die
Existing in our everlasting love

Love has a power that cannot be
Defined, denied nor washed away with the tide
Even if lied to
Love will find a way to

Seek the truth
To tell you and give you
The strength to bring you through
Any difficult time in your life
Or any heartache or strife

Till death do us part
No, not even then
Not even death could destroy
Our love within
For if you die before I
Or I die before you
Our love will still live on through
Through eternity that is
Speaking for both me and you
It will float through air, space and time
Forever it'll be yours and mine
Proclaiming what we once were
Living on forevermore

And so, I recommend this trend
For all of you to partake in
Which will mend your ends
And until then
Love will lead you through the troubled times
And show you all the beauties

Of the earth divine
And will fill your heart, mind and soul
With the worlds sweetest wines
And everlasting joys
That will be yours and mine
How fine our life shall be
As long as love is fixed within
You and me

At moments it may seem like
Love disappears
But don't worry
It will find us again
For you see it only went to
That place where lost love goes
But it'll hear us call out to it
Asking for it to mend our woes
And renew us from our heads
To our toes
And be with us constantly
Within our souls

For I'll love you always
And I know you love me
And together we can be
Happy eternally

But most importantly we'll be loved
And our love shall be everlasting

Final Goodbye

When you said goodbye
I knew it was the last time I would
Hear your sweet voice
The voice that visited me in my dreams
Would no longer make so many favorable
appearances
And I would no longer taste the words
That proceed from your lips
Except for that fateful final goodbye
How I hate that word
The finality of it angers me passionately
Because of that word
You have walked out of my life forever
And forever is how long I will be in
Pain because of it
Wasn't our love supposed to last forever
Until ever
And ever
But goodbye cut it off with a quickness
Shortening forever to today
Because today is the last time I will see you
The last time I will hear you
The last time I will be with you

The last time we will ever be united
Today is all we have
Today is all I have
So let me look at you in this final verse
And remember everything we
Once were
Because once goodbye is spoken
We will be no more
No more, anymore, forever more
I inhale
I exhale
Close my eyes
Take a deep sigh
And render my final goodbye

Plaguing the Mind

Your face is plastered everywhere I turn
Your presence haunts me when I wish to be free
I wish to move alongside the wind
But I am captured in a glass jar
Forced to be stagnant and static
Although I try it is all in vain
It seems that I cannot escape
I cannot escape you
Even though I try
You have me wrapped
Contorted and twisted up in a ball
Of emotions and I seem to be
Constantly unraveling
Whenever you come near
What is this power you seem to have over me
And how do I break free
What spell can be chanted
To dispel this enchantment
In order to release me from
My glass barrier
How do I regain my freedom
How do I retake what was once mine

All of Your Love

You came into my life
Fulfilling me with an overpowering sensation
And I made loving you my newly found occupation
But all too soon I discovered a flaw in the situation
That would equate a worst enemy
Becoming a close relation
It was the application of your heart
That was painful information
Although ¾ of you held me in deep admiration
The other ¼ of your heart contained others
fascination
That seemed to do harm to our foundation
Increasing my frustration
Towards the world's temptation
And materialized congregation
Apart of life's seductive decoration
That has you distracted from our intimate
collaboration
Written in loves legislation
Yes, I may be selfish beyond imagination
But I deserve your complete dedication
And need your whole heart without compensation
Because upon that manifestation

Your presence will send a vibration
Radiating through me without navigation
Colliding with every cell
Sensually healing every wound better then medication
And satisfying me beyond any expectation
And that is why I want
And will settle for nothing less than
All of your love
And that is my final proclamation

End Result

My love for you was a reality
While your love for me was a formality
Held up in court through legality
But disregarding my heart in hospitality
As you make love an abnormality
Causing its mortality
Through your infidelity
Thus, shattering my true love mentality
And causing my emotions to undergo a fatality
That I fear may damage my personality
And disorient its originality
All because of your immorality
And now my state of mind is the unfortunate finality

Unrest

You are a tempest in the night
Whispering your sweet nothings in my ear
I tremble at the sound of your voice
As it stirs the blood within me
I try to run
But you haunt my steps
Lurking in the shadows of my mind
Hiding behind the heartbeat of my desires
Is there no escape from your penetrating
Notions and ideals
Is there no where I can take refuge
And regain my sanity
Or will it forever be overshadowed
By your overbearing dominance
Until I find an answer
I have no choice but to accept that
Which has been forced upon me
And so, I shall be in your company
Again tonight
At the meeting behind the dark of my eyelids

Tainted Love

Loves coat of many colors bleeds red
As I come to terms with the thoughts in my head
Which are tied by society's conscious thread
That has me roped by the neck
Cutting off the circulation to my head
Until I come to my senses
If I want to be wed
And re-evaluate love and the way that my heart is fed
Because his hand is not the one
I am allowed to hold in order to be led
Down loves path of joy and happiness
And all good things said
But instead
I must be strangled and forced to shed
My thoughts on love
Because my thoughts on love are things to dread
And he cannot be with me
Nor me with him
Which is why his heart has fled
And that is the reason why love has bled

Hard Work

It seems like "I'm sorry," is all we ever say
Never minding the season, month or even time of day
Which is why we must fight and
Commence an all out fray
Because at all times hate is the hunter
And love is the prey
Which is why I pray
That you will come to the terms of your way
And see that your selfishness pushes
Me further and further away
Leaving me alone, lost, bitter
And in dismay
As you go off thinking everything is okay
While ignoring my failing emotions
That are soft as clay
And will soon be lost and gone away
Like a needle in a stack of hay
Please forgive the cliché
But all I'm trying to convey
Is that love is supposed to be
A bright, beautiful bouquet
And you my love
Are letting the flowers decay

So, let's not relive the, "I'm sorry's"
Of yesterday
But rather reconnect with love
And promise to cherish and obey
Everything she has to offer, give
And portray
Because she supplies the most
Satisfying pay
That we should spend the rest of our lives
Accepting and working towards
Every single day

Loves Imaginary Hand

He commands attention as he enters
The fire he gives off can melt the next five winters
And every eye is drawn to his perfect face
Because behind it resides heavens infinite grace
He turns around and catches sight of me in the room
And it feels like my breathing may never resume
The crowd parts as he walks in my direction
Complete with poise, charm and perfection
My breath catches in my throat
As my heart speeds up matching the rhythm of a 16th
note

He arrives by my side
And I look at him with my heart open wide
As he softly caresses my cheek
I try not to faint as I listen to the words he readies to
speak
"You are the pulse that sustains my existence
Showing me a new way to live, only through your
assistance
You are the one I have been waiting for
The one created for me to love and adore"

As he wipes away my happy tears
I look at him, preparing to confess what I've been
holding back for years:
"You have always been my one true love
The one I am always thinking of
My love for you will never waiver
When God created you, He did me the ultimate
favor"

He looks at me and smiles so bright
Showing me a glimpse of heavens delight
As he takes a step forward he touches my face
And begins to lower his head at a very slow pace
Welcoming a dream fulfilled that will taste oh so
sweet

But suddenly I am awaken and brought back to reality
And the world reminds me of the state of my
normality
And when I open my eyes
I come to realize
That none of this will ever be
Because he doesn't even see me

Making Today Yours

I dressed up for you
In hopes that our eyes could interlock
If only for a second
So, our paths could not only cross
But wrap around each other
And become entangled around
Our legs
Forcing our limbs to touch
Making the seconds last longer than they should
So, you can fully take in my appearance for you
As I appear before you
Telling you softly that all of this is for you
In hopes of making you feel
Appreciated and loved
But ultimately
Just to make today yours

Love Sick

My temperature is rising
My world capsizing
Nothing no longer is appetizing
And all I keep doing is revising ...

Every single moment we had
Every good joke gone bad
Your new romantic comrade
The fact that I pretend not to be sad

Even though it's all true
The proof is in my chest which I hope you can't see
through
So, I lay in bed with tissue
And tell everyone I have the flu

Six to eight weeks is all I need
Maybe then my heart will no longer bleed
Because you fled from my life with such speed
So now I avoid love at all cost, yes indeed

Happy Birthday

I open my eyes
And you are on my mind
As I hear your voice whisper sweet nothings
And beautiful everything's into my ear
Past conversations swim in my head
And I am reminded of the stroke of your pen
From your stirring poetry
And the constant flowing of your intellect
That moves me closer to you
So, when you unleash our love and attention
For all to see
It will rain down on me
Like manna from heaven
Soaking me through and through
And your bright, shining rays of kindness
Will warm me from head to toe
Drying me off for the first time in my life
And teaching me what it feels like to be beautiful

Your love for God gives me pure joy
And makes me love Him even more
Your discipline and passion frees me
And gives me the courage to admit to you

That my heart may one day me yours

I know it's your birthday
But I feel like God gave me a gift
By allowing me to meet you
So, all I have left to say is
Thank you Jesus!
And Happy Birthday!

Open Up

Knock, knock on my heart
Is it you again?
Why are you still there even after our fight?
You're so good at leaving
But you're even better at coming back

Knock, knock on my thoughts
Why are you everywhere
And how do I make you go away
Your hurtful ways should be the solution
Instead, my love for you is the pollution
That's preventing me from seeing anyone else

Knock, knock on the front door
I unlock it
I lock it
I unlock it
And open it against my better judgement
Because I know you won't stop
And I know I don't want you to
Because your knocks are the only ones for me

Garden of Love

You were forever present
But your presence was hidden in the background
Overshadowed by life's exotic flower
And your own garden of responsibilities
That you tend to everyday with great care
As a good gardener should
But many are not at liberty to do so
Because they choose not to sow what is needed
And therefore cannot reap a harvest
At the correct time or season
But you put in the hard work
And dedication that is required
And for that I admire you
Because of the way you treat others
And your attempts to save the world
One rosebud at a time
And from time to time
I want to let you know
That your efforts are not in vain
And for the first time
Now that I am able to smell the flowers
I see you loud and clear
And what I see

Makes me wish that I had learned
About gardening before now

Craving

You mock me as you stand there
Silently encouraging me on
To supply you with further ammunition
You can fire upon my vulnerable heart

You rejoice in my suffering
Imitating sympathy
When ridicule and judgment
Lie behind the façade

You strangle my love
Cutting off its oxygen
And returning it to me
In an unrecognizable form
You are the destroyer
Of all good my life holds dear
And you perform your job
Without mercy

But a far worst circumstance
Lies not within you
But within me
For it is your presence

That I can't seem to refuse craving
And it is that craving alone
That will be my end

It's You

I take a deep breath to calm my nerves
I lessen my movements to steady my heart
I sit down, relax and let my imagination take over

As I go out tonight, I pretend that it's you
I see your smiling face greeting mine
I envision you opening the car door for me
It is the two of us who chatter nervously in the car
You and I encompass the table for two at a fancy
restaurant
I share the bucket of popcorn with you
As you slide your beautiful arm around my shoulders
We share our first kiss together
Under the luminous glow of the moon
It is you who I want to grow old with
And as I get ready tonight,
I do it all for you

He approaches the porch
Takes a deep breath to calm his nerves
Tries to lessen his movements to steady his heart
He pauses, relaxes and let's reality take over

He had always admired her
But always from afar
Finally filled with courage he prepared to approach
But another asked her out first
Sadness and jealously engulfed him
But with one glance at her face
He felt renewed
And defeat he would not accept
A bribe, an exchange, a trade off dare say was
executed
And now the date he possesses
So now the time had come
And the truth be revealed
With one last breath
He rings the doorbell

I hear the ringing and my fantasies fade away
With one last breath I head towards the door
And upon opening it ...
I see your smiling face greeting mine
My dream has become a reality
For it is you
It has always been you

Love No More

Your love for me has gone away
I feel cold, dry, and led astray
Alone and abandoned in an alleyway
As my friends stare me down like it's judgement day
And the world is unforgiving in a stubborn way
I plead and I apologize, but to my dismay
You have cut me off like the stems of a bouquet
As I learn what if feels like to betray
Our love story is no longer a cliché
My heart is broken and overcome with decay
Because mistakes are deadly and can make you a
divorcee
And steal all your treasure and keep it at bay
I scream for you to hear me on this day
To remake me, remold me like potter's clay
But you are long gone and well on your way
And I will rot alone until my hair is silver and gray
And all I can do now is hope and pray
That your love will return come what may

Across the Room

You commence to make love to me from across the
room
Signaling my attention with the suggestive wink of
your eye
Followed by the slow lick of your lips
As you tongue pauses unnecessarily on the bottom
portion
And your features begin to drip with seduction
As I hear your silent whispers of sweet nothings on
the wind
And I try not to melt into a puddle of mush
At the exchange of our secret loving glances and
forbidden desires
That are ignited from several feet away

But no matter how many feet are between us
Our hidden love affair is the biggest feat we must face
As we exist together on opposite sides of the room
Separated by what seems to be miles of indifference
And feigned association to portray in front of others
And throw them off our trail as we hide our feelings
well

When in close proximity and bury our heated
emotions
While others are present but all that is forgotten
When we share that look from far away
And are at liberty to express our feelings only to
Display them secretly from across the room

Come Back to Me

You were as faithful as the rising of the sun
You were the constant pulse that
Proved breath was within my body
And everybody knew that you were mine
And I was yours

But now,
I can hardly remember your face anymore
It has blurred over the years
Unrecognizable to my eyes
As I try to relive those nostalgic days
And peer back in time
As it appeared to thrive in love

Did we ever exist?
Were we not united as one?
So close that those close
Said our very souls were so intertwined
That if I hit my knee
You would say, "ouch" for me

What has happened?
What evil power have we upset?

For now I feel utterly alone
Blind to the goodness of the world
Locked out without a key

So now I give it to you
I put it all in your hands
I need you to help me
Help me to breathe again
To witness the rising of the sun again
Help me to see
All you have to do is
Come back to me

Eye See Love

In the sea of faces
Yours is the only one I have eyes for
The intensity of your eyes
Binds my heart with love's unwavering
Hands that shake me to my core
Proclaiming loudly
With ardent fervor
Every dream I've ever hoped for
And included a special bonus
Of so much more
The beating of my heart
Is the percussion declaring loves anthem
Announcing to the world its divine powers
And showcasing its rapport
With the entirety of my soul
While simultaneously manifesting
My destiny that is in store
Through your eyes I see loves power
And it has overpowered me now
As I shall be forever bound by your eyes
The eyes of love
The eyes that I adore

Shaking My Hand Tenderly

Vibrant and bright is how I was
Full of life and ready for love
Awaiting your welcoming arms
To open up to me
Embrace me and teach me your
Inner mystery
And our hearts to dance intimately
While we create our own history
And profess our love most frequently
But it will never come to be
For your arms will never embrace me
But only shake my hand tenderly
As if it was an obligation
Performed unconsciously
Instead of an act of admiration
Rendered lovingly

No matter how loud my heart
Cries out to you
You will never hear my soundless tears
Or answer my wordless fears
Alas, they will never reach your ears
Like shears

You cut me unknowingly
Slicing my heart haphazardly
Torturing me relentlessly
All the while smiling friendly
While shaking my hand tenderly

Vibrant and bright is how I was
But now
Now I am left cold and alone
You have left me cold and alone
So next time you try to
Shake my hand tenderly
Don't be mad if I pretend not to see
And try to avoid the whole situation
By turning around to flee
I don't want to be hurt anymore
So please, please
Don't shake my hand tenderly

Thief in the Night

You snuck in through the window
Not making a sound
You searched for the steps
By looking around
You knew what you were after
And you had it all planned out
This would be the greatest heist ever
That people would be talking about
The night was your cover
As you ascended the stairs
The innocent bystander
Knew nothing of your affairs
You approached the bed
With a gleam in your eye
As I lay there dreaming peacefully
Releasing a sigh
You hovered above me
Ready to make your move
I suddenly turned to my side
Throwing you off your groove
Halted for only a moment
You approached me again
Convinced you were the ultimate thief

You knew you would win
You pulled back the covers
And rested your head beside my sleeping form
You wrapped your arm around me
And smiled knowing that this would be the norm
Like a thief in the night
You have taken my heart without my permission
But I am glad
Because now I am in the upmost condition
And realize that love is the best addition

Deny Me Love

Why do you deny me love
Why do you deny me the one gift I so desperately
long for
Crave for
Cry out for
For without love there is no floor to plant my feet
upon
As I open the door to the world before me
Desiring to soar with the eagles above me
As I try to ignore the evils below me
And make light of the pain before me
And bathe in the down pour of my tears
That resurrect from my unspoken fears
That you have brought to fruition
From your hard cold tension
And the fact that you refuse to listen
And as a result have no vision
Because you cannot possibly see
What you're doing to me
While you so casually
Deny me love

I just don't understand

How you can stand in front of me
And knowingly snatch the joy from my heart
I wanted the pleasure to hold you close
But it is you who has hurt me the most
You alone have dashed my hopes and dreams
Cut the thread in my heart at every seam
And so it seems
That you will never reciprocate
This love that I deem necessary to have a worthy fate
But it is a useless debate
And the hour is growing late
So let me question you one last time
With this constant thought
That comes to mind
And even this very moment
I am thinking of
Above all things on this earth
How can you possibly deny me love

Friendship Request

The social network beckons me and I obey
Happily being a willing participant
And making my contributions to the cyber universe
As I stream through the wires
Gathering newsfeed after newsfeed
Of those I dream worthy to be my friend
And my time is spent liking and poking
Commenting and uploading
The small pieces of my so called life
That constitutes my happiness
And mend my sorrows
That I put out there for the world to see
Presenting them a window into my reality
That I feel is not yet complete
And in wanting
Proven by the absence of a certain someone
Not included in my list of friends
Which explains why
My status still reads single
Only because the one
That I want to find me
Seems to have gotten lost
And is wandering out there in space

Searching for me
But not quite knowing where to look
Seeking my face
In the online book
As I hope he will find his way
To my profile
That I have sketched only for him
Knowing that he will
Appreciate the portrait
Because he knows the difference between
Poor traits and good traits
And can accept real art
When others only see blended colors
He uses his heart
And sees a masterpiece
So, until then
I will patiently wait for the happy day
When I will smile
Put my fears to rest and prepare for the best
And finally click accept
To his friend request

I Apologize for Love

Happiness drips off my skin
And shines through my eyes
My eyes
They are big, bright and innocent
I have 20/20 vision
But I'm only seeing now for the first time

My smile lasts hours upon hours
That are stacked so high that
The time keeper wants to fine me
For hoarding blocks of time
But I think he's just jealous
Of the longevity of my joy

Thoughts of you echo in my heart
And are pumped through my entire body
Ensuring that your name
Is etched on every part of me

My feelings for you consume me
Burning me alive with dreams
Of our future life together
And the beauty that is in store for us

Once we join together as one

All is right in the world
And peace and goodwill surround me
Giving me wings to soar
Gracefully in the clouds
Where I am given permission
To be free for the first time in my life

At long last I have discovered
This thing called love
And it's all because of you
So, I step forward to make my confession
But you dash my hopes
Step on my dreams
And break my heart

Your response is:
No, I do not love you
And mine is:
I'm so sorry that I do

Hide and Seek

Your arms are tight
As you hold me close
Your smell is sweet
Embedded within my clothes
My heartbeat quickens
I only hope it soon slows
My knees weaken
I pray it never shows
I shut my eyes
Find my strength
Take a deep breath
One, two, three
Here goes:

I turn my face up to you
Getting lost in the pool of your eyes
Seeing past your pupils
Beyond your tear ducts
And into the depths of your soul
Where the mystery lies
I need to be sure that what I
Hope to be there
Is hiding somewhere inside

Waiting for me to seek it out
And convince it to come top side
Your words and actions hint at its presence
Which fuels me to believe it's real
But I need testimonial evidence
To know truly how it is that you feel
I continue with the search
Looking in every crack and cranny
Hoping to find what I long for
Praying that it will be uncanny
I spot a glimmer of something unusual
Something I've never seen before
It's faint and odd and unknown to me
But it's something I cannot ignore
I examine, touch and press up against it
Trying to decipher what it could be
But with no luck
And plenty of frustration
I just about give up the search and flee
But an idea comes to mind
That will put this thing to the test
And with three words uttered
Either my fears or my joy
Will be laid to rest
I whisper the words
"I love you"

And the curious thing before me
Brings forth a blinding light
You blink back the tears in your eyes
And look at me in such a way
As if you were once blind
And now have regained your sight
I know now that you feel as I do
And will never question it again
Because your love for me is as evident
As the smooth brownness of your skin
"I love you too"
Comes from your mouth
Followed by a beaming smile
Upon your face
Although happy at finding love
It would have been easier on my heart
If it had made its presence
Known in the first place

Minor Adjustments

It begins in a subtle manner
Slow paced and minor so that
I don't notice at first
Gestures I make
Words I say
But the changes are there
And they gradually begin to make
Themselves known as time elapses
The adjustments are made on
A grander scale
Shifts in behavior and personality
And I become so transfixed
Into being this new creation for you
That I lose sight of myself
As I become unrecognizable
And the person I see in the mirror
Is unknown to me
All the while the image you see
Is a familiar sight
From the deep crevices of
Your dreams
Embodying the perfect woman
Without hiccups or failings

So, to you and the
Bureau of adjustments
They were deemed necessary
And you disregard what was lost
No matter how major or minor
The expenses
But you forget about my opinions
In this manner
And that I may not take well to
Being adjusted
And fitted to some dreamlike scenario
Because losing myself
Is not worth the time
Effort or energy
It takes to satisfy you
And your adjustments

Hungry for Love

My tongue salivates at the mention of your name
While the rumble in my belly drowns out everything
But your sweet voice
As I close my eyes and imagine you as food
I wish to devour
And lick my plate clean
Selfishly taking you all for myself
Because I have been fasting for years upon end
That I had forgotten how hungry I was
And never knew what the taste of nourishing food
was like
Nor what it meant to be full
Because my taste buds have only ever been offered
appetizers
But now I crave a full course meal
And only you know how to prepare it properly
So that it leaves me satisfied
And since I have been hungry for so long
I feel as if I could consume you whole
Leaving nothing left
As I want all of you and not just a piece
A child's helping
Or a mere morsel

But all of you absolutely
Completely
And in your entirety
Until my stomach is bursting at the seams
And my tongue can no longer taste
Nor my body no longer ingest
And as my eyes glaze over
Happiness and contentment will be their reflection
Because for the first time in my life
I will understand what it means
To be full from love

Abandoned

The invisible image of you occupies
The empty passenger seat
As I drive, eyes glued to the road
Battling the eerie silence in the car
Void of your comforting chatter
Deprived of your contagious laughter
As I am only left with the
Soundless tunes of the radio
And the constant throbbing
Of my peace of mind
Which is falling away to pieces
That will never be whole again
Because you have left me alone
And will never be here again
Riding beside me
Sitting with me
Listening to me
Standing for me
It seems you want nothing to do with me
And all I can manage to do
Is drive on without you
With the empty passenger seat
Left to remind me of your absence

And your untimely willing departure
That has taken me off course
And caused me to lose sight
Of what's in front of me
As I come to realize
That I have been abandoned
By the one person who I thought knew me best

Coming into Love

Life before you was easy and care-free
You have taken the ease away and reduced it
To a less than tolerable degree
And added your own set of complications
That have destroyed my base of operations
Which controlled the inner workings of my heart
That have been altered and set apart
From the logic of my mind
Which is no longer intertwined
With the new emotions I have been introduced to
Brought upon heavily by you
Which has turned everything upside down
And caused you and I to be the talk of the town
Changing my point of view
And everything about love that I thought I knew
Which I guess is a good thing overall
Because now I know I will always be able to recall
That love may be complex and hard to understand
But overall it is a gift that we all need to demand

Time Wasted

You command my time more than you should
Soaking it up like a sponge
Selfishly leaving me nothing for myself
As the hours tick on
I catch myself waiting for a word from you
Like a lonely child desiring companionship
I allow you more time
Then any one person needs
And as time leaves me behind in the dust
I am still waiting on you
Like a fool waiting to be paid
Who has produced no work
I realize my time has been in vain
Because if you were put
Underneath a microscope
You would never devote the time
To give me a second thought
Let alone the portion of your time
That I so rightly deserve

Love in Question

My days are short
My nights are long
When I try to be with you
Everything seems to go so wrong
But when I stay away from you
Life starts playing a bitter song
So, I am confused
And know not what to do
I want to be happy, loved, protected
And with you is where I want to belong
But if you don't want me
And cannot stand to have me
Then tell me now
Don't mislead me and string me along
In fear that you will hurt my feelings
And as an attempt to prolong
The coming heartache
Because I can take it
Don't let my small frame fool you
I'm really incredibly strong
So, I demand to know the truth
Am I wasting my time by
Staying with you

Or is this thing that we have
Really life long?

Musical Ear

You play me like an out of tune instrument
While your tone-deaf ears refuse to
Recognize the state of misery
The notes are in
As I spoon feed you my
Enthusiasm for music
You regurgitate the harmony
But digest the cacophony of the
Misplayed notes
And you fail to recognize the harsh
Sounds that are being produced
As others cover their ears to the noise
You embrace the sound
Miscalling it music
Not knowing the difference
And not caring what damage it
Does to your instrument
As you refuse invitations to lessons
And advice from well noted
Musicians to help develop your ear
I come to realize that we do not
Share the same taste in music
And I wonder if you will ever

Hear the rhythm of a new tune
As I dare to hope that improvement
Will be made to your perception
Of the worlds wondrous sound
Known as music

Duplicated Love

I wish there were two of you
So I could experience more of you
And take in all of you
Twice the dose to make me feel anew
Sparkling brand new
That is due to the both of you
One of you will replace that which was misplaced
By my mothers hands and flew the coup so to speak
Which changed all that we were used to
But it's fine because we made do
Even when the due date was past
And the morning dew did not last
Because the morning did not want to do anything
Because the morning knew everything it could easily
construe
With its clear view
Which in this world is nothing new
But now with your debut
I can push the button renew
And start a life that can be true
While your twin will pursue
My untamed heart
That's been on hold and long over due

Of drinking loves potion
That only you were meant to brew
But now that you are two
You can fill the empty void
Which I can bid adieu
While at the same time
I can grow old with you
Forever loving you like I do
Multiplying my love by two
Which is how it goes out of me
And into you

Hesitant Love

You said you love me more than I know
But what do I know about love
Other than the afterglow
The truth is that I really know nothing
Except for what you've shown me
And told me
And allowed me to see
But what experience do I really have
With this happy-go-lucky view
To know if what you say is true,
Honest and not something new
You have to remember that this is
Unfamiliar territory for me
But I know that you are well versed
And well traveled in this arena
So don't laugh at me for my ignorance
Like a spotted hyena
Please forgive me if I hesitate
When you tell me about your constant
Undying love for me
But how do I really know
If my love and your love agree
And that when it boils down to it

Your love will not flee
I guess that I'm just really shaky
About this thing called love
Because it's something I've
Never really gotten ahold of
Or see the likes of
That is until ... dare I say it
Dare I admit it
Until ... well, only time will tell
And in the future we shall see
What will unfold
But as of right now
My love is on hold

Over It

I no longer have a taste for your lips on my tongue
For that craving has been scattered in the wind
Along with your scent that would linger on me for
hours
Without end
For it was hours that once passed by
That held only thoughts of you
Keeping my mind occupied on
Anything but you was my most difficult occupation
But now the job has been simplified and abbreviated
With you out of the picture
And although it may appear void
With your presence now gone
The image of my hand holding
An empty space from the cut out version of you
May seem sad and depressing
But in your absence I have
Found strength
And rediscovered my focus
Which has shifted from you and
Is now placed on me
And it is here in this place
That I find I can make it

Without you

My Name

Your lips purse together
In strong determination
Then release without the least bit of hesitation
While simultaneously the sound
Expels in order to pursue its obligation
That comes into manifestation
As your tongue caresses your
Mouths inner decoration
And the letters come into formation
Sending forth a tantalizing sensation
Which forces my breathing to
Tremble with anticipation
And causes within me a vibration
Where upon I shake and quiver
Without shame
All due to the way
The lovely way
That you say my name

Love Gone Wrong

Angry breath
Expelled from my mouth
Forced through tight lips
Held in place by clenched teeth
And a stubborn jaw
My eyes dart around the room
Leaving bloodstained trails of images
Behind in bold crimson coating
My lungs fill with frustration
Impeding my better judgment
as I realize my emotion
through my actions
and demonstrate my anger to those
innocent bystanders encircling me
forgive me in advance
for under these circumstances
I am not liable for what I may do
You have been prewarned
Because mismanaged love
Can produce a woman scorned

More Than Gold

The love for your pets was what drew me in
The affection you gave them made the journey begin
My heart took note of the things I saw
Your kindness, your patience, your ability to be raw
You cradled the cats tenderly with care
Showcasing your love in the open with me there
Your playfulness with Max was fun and entertaining
The dad vibes you gave made your portrait the
ultimate painting
My desire to be around you mirrored the pets
Your energy and essence are all assets
I realize now how much you mean to me
My admiration for you is something that will never
flee
My heart is open for whatever comes my way
Because falling for you has made me happier than I
can say
So, the moral of the story if I can be so bold
Cats, dogs and love, if I can have all three
That's worth more than gold

Love in Vain

My love for you makes no mark on your heart
For my intentions are pointless
And there is no point
Much less a reason
To go out of my way to please you
Because your affection for me
Is shown less and less
Dwindling to meager forms
Which will eventually result to nothing in your eyes
And nothing in my heart
Which is shown by its splitting into two halves
And then breaking into pieces
And ultimately never being whole
Just like my smile
Smashed
Chipped
And barely recognizable
As I grin only to reveal
A miserable excuse
Of a lopsided frown
With too many missing gaps
To be called a smile
And yet, I still smile

Only for you
In hopes that you will eventually come around
And sweep me into your arms
As you mend my broken smile
With your kisses
And heal my damaged heart
With your love
That I desperately long for
And am willing to return to you in ten-fold
As I stand to the side
Waiting to thrust my love upon you
At the slightest of hints
Willing to give you all of me
At the drop of a hat
Longing to love you
The way the word was designed to be used
Applying it to every application
And in every capacity possible
Only waiting for a single word from you
A single glance
A single gesture
To give you all I've ever dreamed of giving someone
Holding nothing back
But I fear that I will be waiting forever
Because I love you in vain
And you will never be able to return my love

Whose strength is only met with your indifference
Whose ardent fervor is only met
With your nonchalant attitude
And although I try to mail you the letter addressed to
Eternally yours
My dear sweet love
All my heart and more
And signed
Unconditionally
Lovingly
Fondly
Passionately
Forever yours
Your only reply is
Return to sender
And nothing more, and nothing less
So now I do the only thing I can do
I take my dysfunctional heart
And tormented smile
And stand in the shadows
Determined to wait for you
And hope that one day
You will learn to love me
Because if you do
Then all the pain that I have suffered
Will be worth it in the end

At Long Last

Your body is flawless
Your words are vast
My gaze is fixed on you
My heart is beating fast

You softly kiss my hand
My emotions are on full blast
I stare into your eyes
And forget all about my past

I feel myself falling
Flailing like an outcast
When suddenly you catch me
As I've found love at long last

Love's Failed Attempt

We knew from the beginning
How it would be
The way that it would go
The pain that would come
But we ignored it
Like the approaching clouds before a storm
We ignored it
Offering welcome instead of seeking sanctuary
We ignored it

It was only a matter of time
Before reality caught up to us
The sprinter can ignore the pain
For only so long before his knees give out
And our knees have buckled beneath us
Crumbled and come crashing down
Like a falling tree with a scream of timber
Our knees have given out
Unable to stand
Unable to be strong
Our knees have given out

But all this was seen

We saw the dark before the light
We knew the failure would come
That the love would leave
Like a gust of wind
Never to return
Our precious love
Our precious love is gone
Never to return
Lost to the emptiness of the night
Floating beyond our reach
Never to return

The Ultimate Gift

How frequent will you visit?
How often will you stay?
I wish to see you every morning
And the hours throughout the day
I welcome your approach
And your constant unwavering hand
I rejoice in your goodness
And the forever golden band
You unite two people
For better or worse
With you they are able to endure
And overcome the evilest curse
I hope to see you soon
Because to me you are so dear
I know I will be at peace
If only to keep you near
I look forward to your coming
I hope your arrival will be swift
Because it is you I wait for
You alone would be the ultimate gift

Distance

Your face was so close to me
That I could feel your breath
But out of nowhere
I was jerked back
Separated from you
Beyond my reach
With no explanation
But just matter of fact
I was left heart broken
And crushed
Now I stand at a distance
Stretching forth my hand
To brush across your face
But not coming anywhere close

We are far apart
And I don't know how to close
The gap between us
Getting us within
Arm's length once again

Loves Possibility

You caught my eye
In a crowd of strangers
Drawing in all my attention and interest
As I followed your actions willingly
Listened to your conversations surprisingly
And smiled to myself knowingly
All the time imagining a future for
You and me
A paradise of love
That I know we can share
With sands of passion
And waves of admiration
That I can feel
Not only in my dreams
But in reality
A life full of love between you and me
Me and you
And even though you may be
A stranger among strangers
You have been singled out
Brought into focus
While the background has become blurred
And I know that it is you

I have been waiting for
Patiently hoping for
And now you stand before me
In the world's most public arena
That I bypass everyday
And on today I find you
Amongst the world's population
But in loves population
There is only you and I
The two of us remaining
Rejoicing in love
And looking forward
To all its wonderous possibilities

Never Again

I cried out to you amongst the darkness
But you turned a deaf ear to my struggle
Ignoring my pains
And blocking out my suffering
Bypassing more than my malcontent
But my state of existence
What a fool you have made of me
Mocking my falsehood of joy
Sending a charlatan to marry us
By the vows of stupidity
While your eyes dance with amusement
At your indiscretion
My heart has been poisoned
And was nearly strangled by the
Incredulous hands of doubt
But my mind has been made clear
The misty haze is gone forever
I have learned
I have lost
And I shall never love again

Dissecting Love

With the sharp blade of truth
I slowly make the incision
Down the center
Causing a rift between
Profound joy and complete selflessness
I peel back the flaps of the entity
Revealing a blinding light
That sweeps over me
Like a wave upon the sand
As my eyes adjust
And the brightness subsides
I see into its core
A swirl of colors dance around
As if to a tune of an unheard melody
They filter into the room
Through the gaping hole I just administered
My fingers probe the insides
To unearth its secrets
Through my gloved fingers I encounter
Smoothness smoother than silk
And softness softer than furs
I search for the center
The brain

The master behind this thing
This emotion
This mystery
I gather my surgical equipment
And all my aides for assistance
I have to find the source behind this power
I pull
I cut
I analyze
I decipher
And then I see it
Not visually
But sensuously
It's as if a nuclear bomb has gone off inside me
But without the damaging repercussions
I can feel love pulsating through my veins
I can see its vapors riding on the coat tails
Of my breath
I can feel it shining through my eyes
And bouncing off every item my vision encounters
I have never known anything so powerful
So, this is love
This immense pleasure and
Overwhelming exuberance
There are tears in my eyes
And I don't know why

I touch the salty wetness
And even there I can feel the love
It cannot be explained
It cannot be dissected
It just is
And will always be
Love
Simply, love

Reality Check

I search for you in the dark
I seek your face in the night
Only to grope around blindly
Grasping nothing but air and emptiness
As I stumble around the room
Colliding into discarded unknowns
Easily bruising from the unintended contact
While being denied the sense of touch
I require from you
So, I keep roaming the shadowy prison
Longing to feel you out
And experience skin on skin once again
Again
And again
And again that thought drives me on
Propelling me forward
Not into clarity but into ignorance
As the distance between my feet and
The truth become greater
To the extent that if the lights turned on
Filling the room with beams of reality
Your absence would be noted
But more than that

I would see that your presence
Had never once graced the room to begin with

Loves Fiery Passion

Your name was whispered in the wind
Igniting my senses like a strike to a matches end
As I feel engulfed by the flames of desire
That keeps creeping up higher and higher
All caused by the mere thought of your voice
Teaching me that a life of love is my only choice
I feel the fire burning relentlessly
Consistently
Persistently
And fundamentally always on
On your name
On your voice
On your body
On you
I close my eyes and see your face
And I lay down to give my emotions space
To roam and feel and flaunt and explore
It's like a bomb has gone off blasting me through an
open door
Jolting through me suddenly
As I feel overwhelmed from the intense heat
That the thoughts of you bring
And I extend my hand further into the furnace

Where my heart now resides
And I ascend to the core of the blaze
Where our souls collide
As I try to comprehend
This incessant burning and yearning
That has taken over
And refuses to descend
From the state which I am in
And I know we shall spend
Every moment here together
In loves fiery passion
Forever and ever

Anniversary

Our first date will always stand out
It was magical, beautiful and special without a doubt
Your conversation
Our mutual infatuation
My elation
From meeting someone so perfect
And full of respect
No wonder love soon took affect
I got lost in you
My understanding of relationships is askew
I was too brand new
And after awhile you hit undo
Leaving me alone
Thrown
And in the unknown
Which is where I stay
Sad and held at bay
By my memories of that very first day
That I saw your face
And can't seem to erase
No matter time or space
My love doesn't want to leave your embrace
Even though I've been replaced

And my heart has been disgraced
For holding on so tightly
And you tried to be so knightly
And I wouldn't budge even slightly
And now I contritely try to
Express how I feel
With wounds so large they may never heal
And my Achille's heel has been my love for you
Which is unreal
And as the months peel
And today is revealed
And I with no shield
No longer concealed
Am bloody and beaten and dying
On a battlefield
What an ordeal
I need open heart surgery
Just to survive our anniversary

Love's Debut

You were a fairy tale
Too perfect to be true
You found me among thousands
And messaged me out of the blue
Your profile drew me in
And your message was beautiful too
You talked of God and dreams
And had such a rare point of view
After the first two weeks
I was more than smitten
Dare I say, I was falling for you
Your words took my breath away
And the feelings you evoked turned
My insides to goo
My heart was taking over
And my logic was saying adieu
Who knew I could feel this way
Without ever seeing you
But with your power to woo
And my hearts desire
And the closeness we came to
I knew my feelings were not untrue
It's you that I've been

Waiting for
Hoping for
Praying for
Don't you see, you've come to my rescue
You make me feel beautiful, special
And one of a kind
And that's just a sneak preview
I know God, love and our dreams
Will see us through
So, with a kiss and a promise of forever
I smile and tell God, "Thank You!"

Bleeding Heart

The air whips through the hole
you bore into my heart
Sending forth an echo of agony
through the four chambers
That threaten to collapse
Shirking their responsibilities
And resigning from their duties
Which would halt the flow of blood
That is already seeping out of
The break of my fractured organ
That you have breached and punctured
With your cruel words
And hurtful actions
That have robbed me of my time
My energy
And now it seems of even the oxygen
That resides in my blood
And gives life to my body
That nobody was supposed to be
Able to break
But only enhance by making my heart
Swell with love and affection
But instead you have severed

That connection
And caused me unimaginable pain
Which pains me with every breath
That I take
Forcing my damaged ticker
To function in a pool of blood
As if a gunshot victim left at the
Scene of a crime
All because you committed the crime
Of breaking my heart
And worst of all
You just watched
And did not try to stop the bleeding

Unknown Love

Why didn't I see you before
Why am I just now finding you
When you've been here the whole time
You were tossed in a sea of faces
And you cried out to me
But I did not hear
You are the fish that is worth catching
But I was using the wrong bait
How could my ears go deaf
To your soothing beautiful voice
It was so strong and clear
How could my eyes bypass
Your vibrant smile that was
Constant and dignified
I want to start anew
I want to start fresh and clean
Because for the first time I see you
I see you loudly
And you are beautiful to me
I know I've known you for a few years now
But can I meet you
Can I know you
Can I love you

Slow Death

I see the words addressed to someone else
And I know I should not have read them
But I did with a heavy heart
And I smile at the words not meant for me
Feigning my sadness to the outside world
And keeping my emotions locked up inside
For the name I see is not my own
But belongs to that of another
Whose memory brings pain to my heart
Ever since the day I watched
The pain cry out on your face
The first time you told me about her
And her past transgressions
Commenced upon your heart
And after all of that I wonder
How could you have written those words
Of love for her
As I stare at the gift you show me
How could you want to go back to her
After all the pain she caused you
When it is I who held you close
And wiped away your tears
It is I who has been here for you

It is I who has listened to you
It is I who has stood by your side
And now you tell me that you want
To go back to her
And your ticket is this gift
And these kind words
That I so desperately wish were
Meant for me
And as you look up at me
You smile that smile of yours
That makes everything right in the world
And I have no choice but to be a good friend
Swallow my own desires
Put yours first
Hide my undying love for you
Give you a hug
And allow you to go back to the
Woman that does not love you

See Me

You are the pleasure of the sand between my toes
You are the beauty of a sunrise
And the majesty of a sunset
You are the cool breeze on a hot summer day
To me you are amazing in every possible way
You are loved by many
Especially by me
Perhaps one day I'll be able to tell you
I'll be able to let you see

The Loss of Love

I come to you in the night
Dressed to impress in heavenly delight
Aimed to please you and all your senses
Having no care of the expenses
Wanting your favor and pleasure to be high
As I slowly approach with a gleam in my eye
My heels click against the hard wood of the floor
As I know in my heart that you will be
The only one I adore
I give you my biggest smile and walk forth boldly
But am suddenly halted as those eyes hit me coldly
The pupils of a woman who is not me
She is standing in the place that I long to be
I stand still as if frozen in time
And you look at me as if I had committed a crime
I was only trying to show that my love for you is true
But now I see that my dreams with you will never
debut
The words of rejection are not needed
Because your face says it all
And so, I turn quickly
Taking my leave and hoping not to fall
My room is a comfort to my

Embarrassment and misery
And makes a good place for me
To cry relentlessly
The pain I feel is vast and demanding
Because my heart is now broken
From my newfound understanding
You never loved me as I hoped you would
Your kindness and sincerity was
Completely misunderstood
I put my heart out on the line
By wearing my emotions on my sleeve
And now I am alone
And fear the burden of sadness
Will never leave
So much for my fairy tale
So much for my happy ending
I have nothing left
My heart is too heavily broken for mending
But in that chance I took
Although hurtful it has been
The truth was revealed about our future
Concluding that our love will never win

In Your Dreams

Peace exudes from you
As sleep engulfs you
And I am pulled into you
By the hands of the sandman
That allows me to enter your dreamland
Which is a land I've dreamed of
Hoping that it would exist solely for
The two of us
Which makes me smile
Even as I begin falling through the
Spaces of your mind
And am awakened in a field of
Bright colors
Which force my eyes to adjust
Enabling me to see more than
Black and white
And in a way gives me a new found sight
That I embrace
As I look towards the heavens and see
Clouds of gold fill the sky
And wonder out loud if they rain
Rubys and diamonds
And hope one day you will give me the latter

But that is a matter for another dream
Which is typically the subject of
My own reoccurring fantasy
But now back to your dream
That I have stealthy invaded
As I now see you standing next to me
And you draw me into your arms
Pulling me closer than I've ever been
Your skin to my skin
Your breath to my breath
Your thoughts to my thoughts
Tighter and tighter
Closer and closer
To you, in you, through you
Until I am familiar with
Every body part
Ever emotion
Every heartbeat
Everything about you and everything about me
Has been interchanged from this embrace
And I see you
As I have never seen you before
Now understanding
How you really feel about me
And as you open your eyes
You see me sitting there

Having enjoyed watching you sleep
But above all else
Knowing that your dreams
Are full of the love
That you have for me

Another

My feet stop in mid motion
As your eyes look to another
My breath catches in my throat
As you move close to another
My body goes ice cold
As you kiss another
My heart explodes
As I have been replaced by another

The Strength of Love

We stand before the alter hand in hand
The wedding band ready upon command
As the happenings before me are more
Then I've ever dreamed of
More than I could have planned
I don't even hear the concert band
Or notice the layout of the land
For in you I have found my promised land
And I am finally ready to take that stand
As I have come to understand
That this beautiful power of love is at hand

As we stare deeply into each other's eyes
There is something that we both fail to realize
That there is an evil out there disguised
In lies and full of goodbyes
Whose sole mission is to see that our love dies

For when I'm ready to say, "I do"
The world responds, "You don't have a clue"
When I'm ready to declare my admiration
Respect and love
The world says, "No, none of the above"

When I'm ready to say, "Till death do us part"
The world is ready to break my heart

The world is against us
And we are against the world
That only means that we have to
Love harder
Have trust longer
And forgive better
We have to prove to the world
And make a declaration to all
That marriage can stand tall
And is as secure as a concrete wall
And with the proper care
Love will never fall

Bamboozled

Don't believe the hype
Dismiss the warm fuzzy feelings
Disregard the smiles and kind words
Divert the blushes and all emotions
To areas of greater consequence
Deferment is not enough
For love must be eradicated
Absolutely from all aspects that sustain life
Trust me on this
And heed my advice
Never, ever, ever
Love

Goodbye My Lover

Heavy footsteps turn away from me
As you walk further and further away from me
Leaving me behind with nothing for comfort but a
broken heart

I force myself to watch
Wanting to cry out to you
My watery eyes linger upon you
Desperately wanting relief
But keeping silent
Having hope
But knowing the truth
Knowing the terrible truth
And the cold feeling of isolation

We'll never be together again
Our footsteps will never again stride in unison
Only separately and in different directions

Will you remember what we once had
Will you have any recollection of me at all
Or will our memories drift away
As you are drifting away from me now

I think of all this as I watch you
I bury my tears in the dirt
Letting the dust sweep them away

I shall cry no more
I shall cease my grieving
And force my heart to mend itself

Now I shall turn around and walk towards a new life
But with one last look
And one last tear
I say
Goodbye, my lover

Beginning

The innocence of our beginning
Was sweet and tender
Like holding hands for the first time
It was warm
New
And gave me fuzzy feelings
That I want to experience
Time and time again
But only with you
And you alone
Because you have introduced me
To this mysterious world of
Romance and affection
You selected me out of the crowd
When no one else saw me
And you were the ultimate gentleman
The whole way through
Caring for me tenderly
And guiding me slowly
Which made you more attractive
To my eyes
And solidified you in my heart
And because of that

I shall never forget you
And the moments we've shared
Will last forever

Abused Love

Your anger steams like smoke from a train
Only making itself known in my presence
While you build up the façade in front of others
It is I who receives the blows they deserve
It is I who is the recipient of your anger
When no one else is around
And my innocence is a useless coat of armor
When you are in an irate state
I dodge the hits to no avail
As I try to recover from the slap
You just dealt me
And my shame makes the contact even harder
As I stomach the after effects
Of your disagreeable actions
That I must bear in the misnomer of love
But as time progresses
And your behavior remains unchanged
The name of love becomes tattered
Withered and beaten
And before I know it
Love has become just as abused as me
Unrecognizable and without
Form or meaning

For it was lost along the way
Unable to be held together by bandages
Not capable of rescuing with first aid
Hopeless to reconstruct with medical attention
Because abused love is not love at all
And that realization
Is my freedom from this situation

One Day

Little girl fantasies
Happily ever afters
The knight in shining armor
Do you like me yes or no
Pinterest wedding photos
Here comes the bride
Here comes the lies

Love on the brain
Love in the heart
Love on the screen
Love in the books
Love in my dreams
Love all around
Love can't be found

Biding my time
Waiting for my season
Looking towards heaven
Waiting by the phone
Time ticks on
My youthful days are gone
The calendar turns

Celebrities come and go
But I have nothing to show
It's just me and my ideas of love
Hoping that one day they will be realized

Blinded by Love

One. My words betray me
Two. My actions make a fool of me
Three. My apologizes are old news to me
Time and time again I fall victim to
One, two and three
Which wears you down constantly
And frustrates you hopelessly
When all I desire is for you to see
My love for you
Which I keep on display for all to see
Not ashamed for others to know
That my love is a guarantee
And has acted as a key that has
Set my emotions free
Giving me the incentive needed to
Love you passionately
Without judgement and unconditionally
Which is why I try to be soothing
To you as a palm tree
But instead have become more like
A dead sea
That kills you more and more
Relentlessly

Whenever my emotions get
The better of me
Causing me to be blind and
Preventing me to see
That you and I will never be
No matter how much I want us
To be we
You will be you
And I will be me
And the only way we can exist is
Separately
Which is something that even a
Blind man can see
So why is it so difficult for me

Letting Go

My grasp was tight
You held me close
I breathed you in
Then started to do the most

My heart was open
And you were kind
I had everything I wanted
You were always on my mind

The days were short
The nights were long
I fell for you so quickly
I just didn't know it was wrong

My calls increased
My expectations grew
You put up with a lot
I never considered your view

The change was slow
But it was there
I chose not to see it

And you chose not to share

I love you, I love you
Came out of my mouth
It didn't fix things at all
Just made them go south

Your feelings had changed
I wasn't sure why
This was quite a predicament
But I didn't want a goodbye

My feelings are valid
And yours are too
The relationship was fading
That much I knew

We talked it out
First me then you
We reached an agreement
And then we withdrew

The end was here
We went our separate ways
You went to the left
While I took one more gaze

My memories are happy
My heart is sad
Our relationship is over
But I can't be mad

I watch and I watch
Until you disappear
Knowing that I am alone
Does not make me fear

Letting you go
Was a hard lesson to learn
But with application and growth
One day love will return

Old School Love

What happened to that love our grandparents had
Those tender moments expressed
With sincere gladness
That fought off the sadness
While rebuking the madness
That the world would conjure up
Enough to make the heavy weight champion
Look like a chump

Those long-ago days when
Divorce wasn't an option
And life struggles an adoption
You had to adapt to
And suffer through
But all awhile you both knew
That although the complications brew
You would hold on steady and strong
For however long
It took for the unbearable wrong
To transform into a forgivable sing along

Why can't we relive the past
When our strength surpassed temptation

And our trust was last to give in
And kept abreast with our
Respect for each other
That would always holdfast amongst
Our vast love affair
That would be our best and our last

I want that love to return
That unfailing love between two people
That could not be torn asunder
But only admired in wonder
While under our grandparents
Point of view
It was a view worth having
And worthy to pursue
Because true love will always
Get you through

You

My heart cries out to you
But there is no response from you
I wish you would put me before you
Why can't I stop loving you?

Love Found Me

I saw her in your eyes
And I smiled
I knew she would come
I'm just glad the day has finally arrived
I used to believe she was upset with me
As I wondered what had I done to anger her
What crime could cause such detachment
What hatred could result in such unfulfillment
What act could leave me void
But alas, no more
For she is here, in you
And for that I am happy
I am loved

Comparison

You look at me
And all you see is her
As another face moves forward
Blending in with mine
Twisting and turning
Meshing and molding
Until I am no longer visible
No longer present
No longer me
The me is gone
The you is there
And the her is now all you have
All that you want
Kicking me out
Not letting me in
Taking over my body without
My permission
Changing my hobbies, quirks
And ambitions
Forcing me into submission
And sentencing me to death
Because you always liked her best
And when she didn't want you

You found me
And when I didn't compare
You had an affair
But not with just anyone
With her
The only one who ever existed
The her who you created
Inside of me
Because when you look into my eyes
No matter how loud my cries
All you see are the lies that you painted
Which makes her full size
So, lets surmise that
I am not the prize
And this is my demise
As I finally realize
That you never wanted me

Saying No to Love

The gleam in your eye
Informs me that it's time for me to go
The dam has been broken
And my emotions begin to flow
My heart and my brain made a pact long ago
For a time described in this scenario
In which my brain would take command
And my heart would lie low
Allowing me to hold back
And take it slow
Vacate the premises after saying no
And withdraw my application
From love's game show
Because I've been hurt too many times
Blow after blow
Always saying yes
And never saying no
Lining my heart with so much woe
Afraid I was going to die
And turn up as a Jane Doe
And death by love isn't the best thing
To undergo
Just ask Romeo

Oh wait, you can't ... hello!
You know, love is supposed to be
Like winning the lotto
But it's also like being swept up
By a tornado
So, which is it?
Eh, tomato, tomahto
But as for me
I know which way to go
No longer will I have to tiptoe
I will just say no
And successfully escape from the
Throes of love's glow

Lifelong Impression

One day
One encounter
One moment in time
Is all it took ...

For you to press upon me
The soft touches of admiration
And impress me with your level of respectfulness
And full-on access to all of your attention
Thoughts and kindness
That is delivered with finesse
And opens my eyes to this romantic process
And in you I see love's success
As you imprint on my heart
And your lifelong impression
Will live on in me in excess
As I come to a point where I'm finally able to confess
That my love for you is something
I happily and forever will express

Fading Away

My actions are in vain
As you have the attention of another
My words of admiration
Bounce off your ears
As you have selective hearing for a
Voice not my own

The love in my heart
The loudness of my quiet
The passion within my touch
Has no effect on you for you see me not

I scream your name
I make a raucous
I push with all my might
But it's to no avail
For you see me not

I am a lonely flower
In the field of dreams
And you no longer fancy my petals
Which is making my roots feel like
They are becoming undone

And now my biggest fear is being
Done unto me
Because I am disappearing
Before your eyes
As if I'm in a magic act
As the unsuspecting volunteer
To prove the power and magnify
The illusion of love
That is being drained from my heart
As the magician declares:
Now you see me
But now you don't

And poof, I am gone from you
Even though I'm standing right next to you
Covered by the shadow of another woman
Like a black cloak used in the act
That makes me act in a manner not my own
All due to the unfairness of love
That is crippling me
And making me question
What I was originally taught
For you no longer love me
Made evident because you see me not

Lovely

You came in an unlikely form
Showing your face to my ready eye
I almost glanced right over you
And walked right on by
But then something stopped me
Or rather it was you who caught me
With an invisible beam and a soundless scream
That only I could redeem
All apart of loves confusing regime
That the two of us now follow faithfully
As we have faith fully
In all that we do
And everything we want to pursue
As we realize love is what matters
Just look
Love is what brought me to you

EPILOGUE

Love is a journey filled with many ups and downs. There is joy, pain, confusion and beauty amongst its path. I've been writing poetry since I was in high school and have always been drawn to express my thoughts about love in this particular format. Thank you for taking this journey with me and for reading my words. I hope they have been as helpful to you as they have been to me. May we all find and experience the absolute best parts of love.

ABOUT THE AUTHOR

Ashley Davidson is an Atlanta native who thrives on movies, books, kindness, storytelling and inspiration. She is an actress, writer, filmmaker and adventurer who loves spending time with her family and growing in artistic endeavors.

She would like to offer a gracious THANK YOU to anyone who purchases any of her books!

Feel free to connect with her on social media!
Instagram: @iashleydavidson
Twitter: @iashleydavidson
TikTok: @iashleydavidson
YouTube: Ashley Davidson